EXPI
KINDNESS

From the
Exploration Kindness
Series

Exploration Kindness

Sue Albanese   Dawn Koltiska   Coleen Thurber
Illustrated by Partho Roy

Part of the
Exploration Kindness Series

Published by EK Publishing
Denver, Colorado

Copyright © 2024
Sue Albanese, Dawn Koltiska, Coleen Thurber, & Partho Roy
All Rights Reserved

ISBN: 979-8-325883-85-9 (paperback)

DEDICATION

We dedicate this book to the ever wonderful and forever magical soul of Megan Koltiska. Megan was the epitome of kindness and was a guiding, bright light to all who were lucky enough to know her. While she blessed this world with her beautiful presence for 31 years, her life was about love, kindness, and indeed exploration - living to the absolute fullest while she was with us.

We know she would have loved all that Exploration Kindness stands for.

Hi! My name is Zuri. My name means "good" and "beautiful".

I love art and music.

I wear clothes that are bright and most of the time don't match.

I'm so glad you decided to join me today!

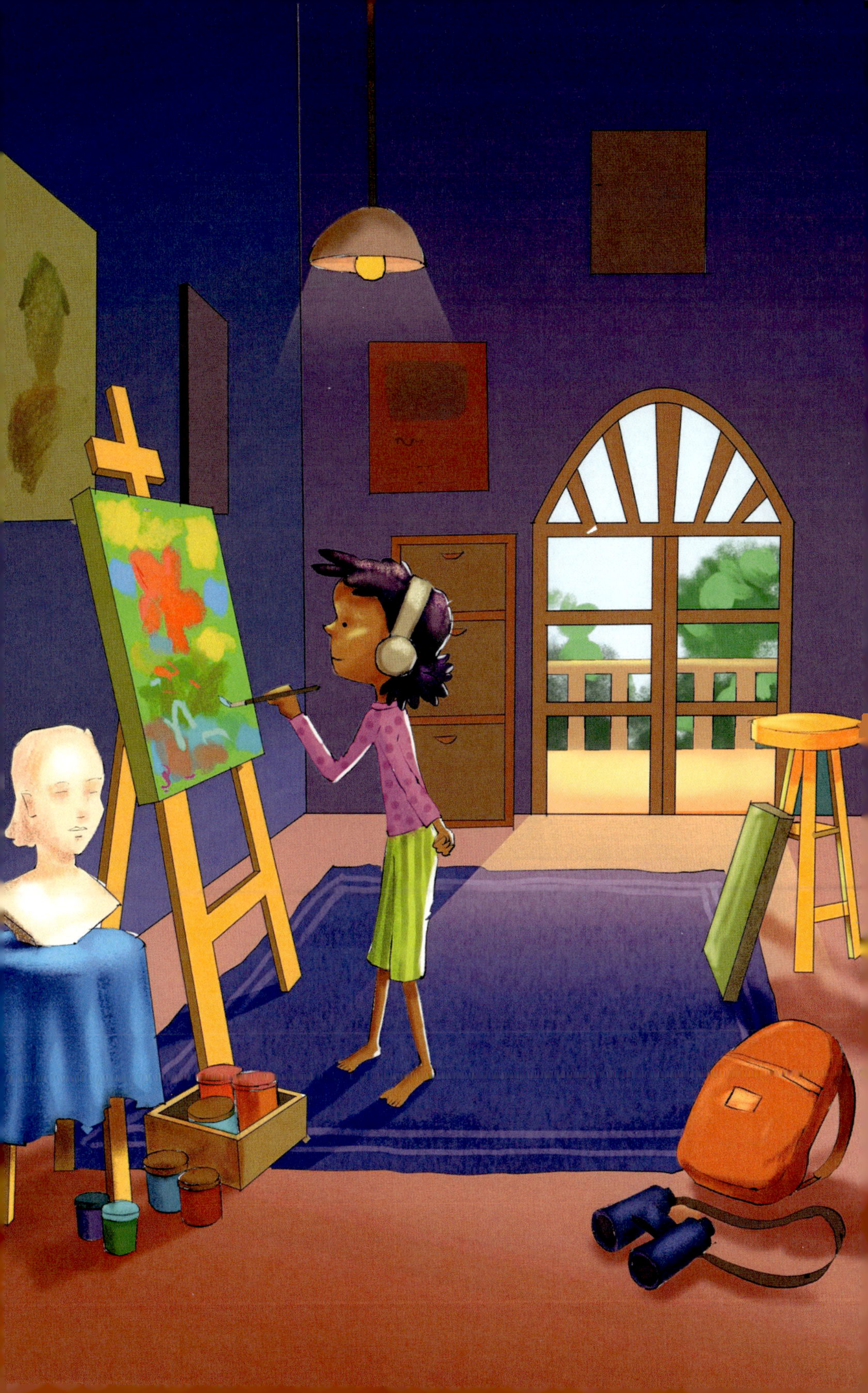

This is my friend, Liam.

His name means "strong" and "resilient".

Liam loves basketball and hanging out with his friends.

Oh...by the way... What's your name?

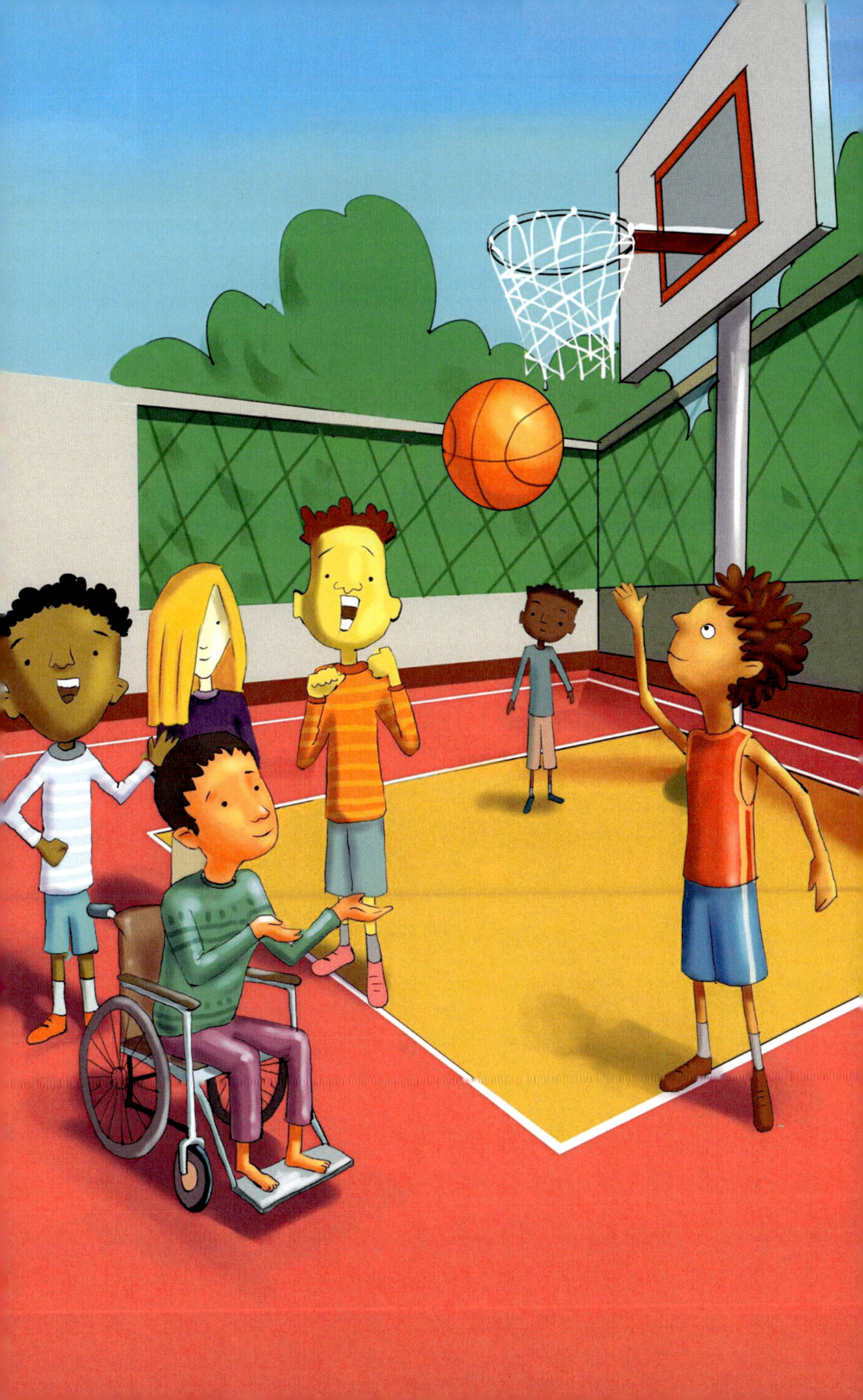

Liam and I are explorers.

Today we are exploring kindness!

Do you know what kindness is?

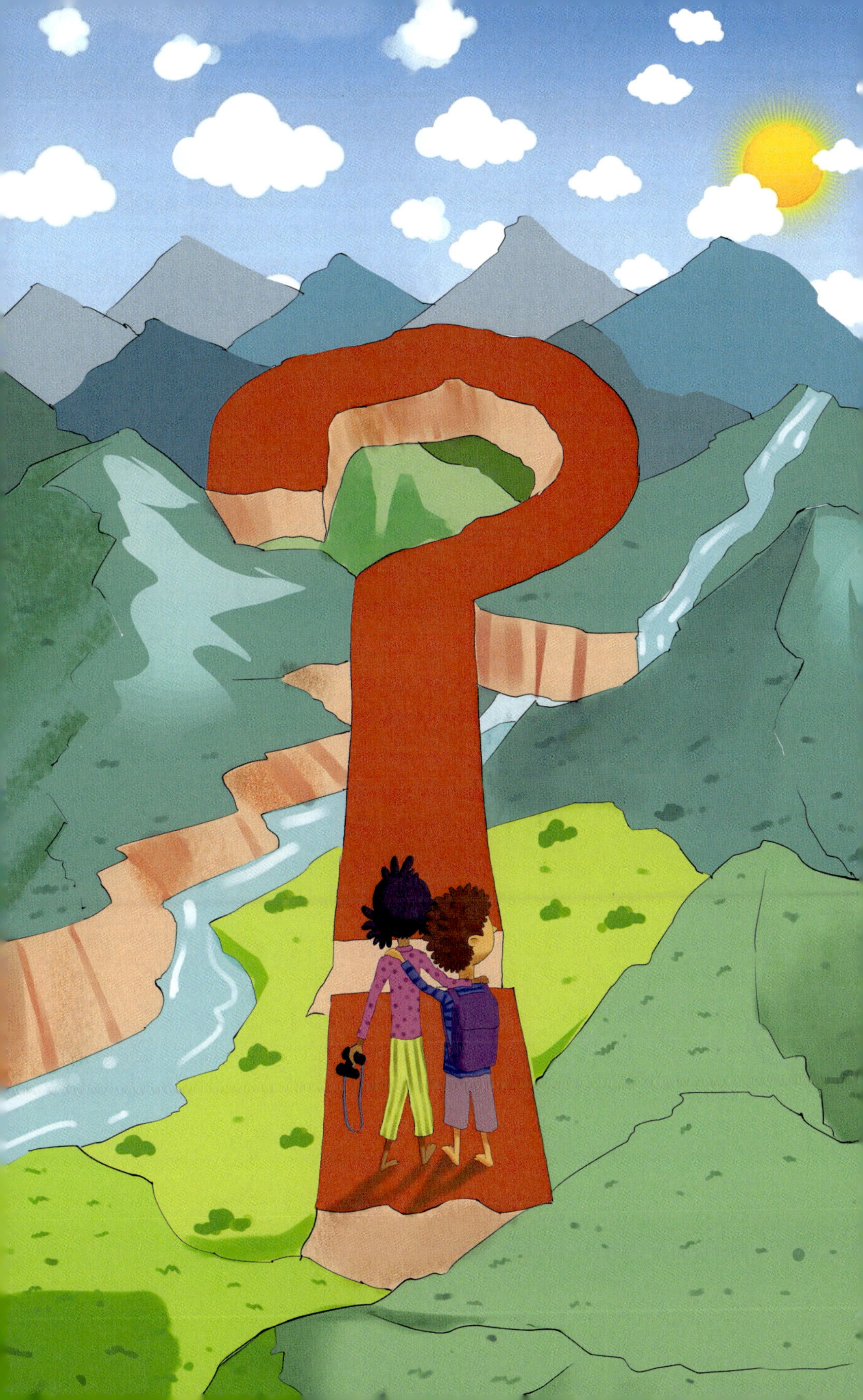

We sure didn't know at first, so we asked some people what they thought kindness meant.

Do you want to hear what they said?

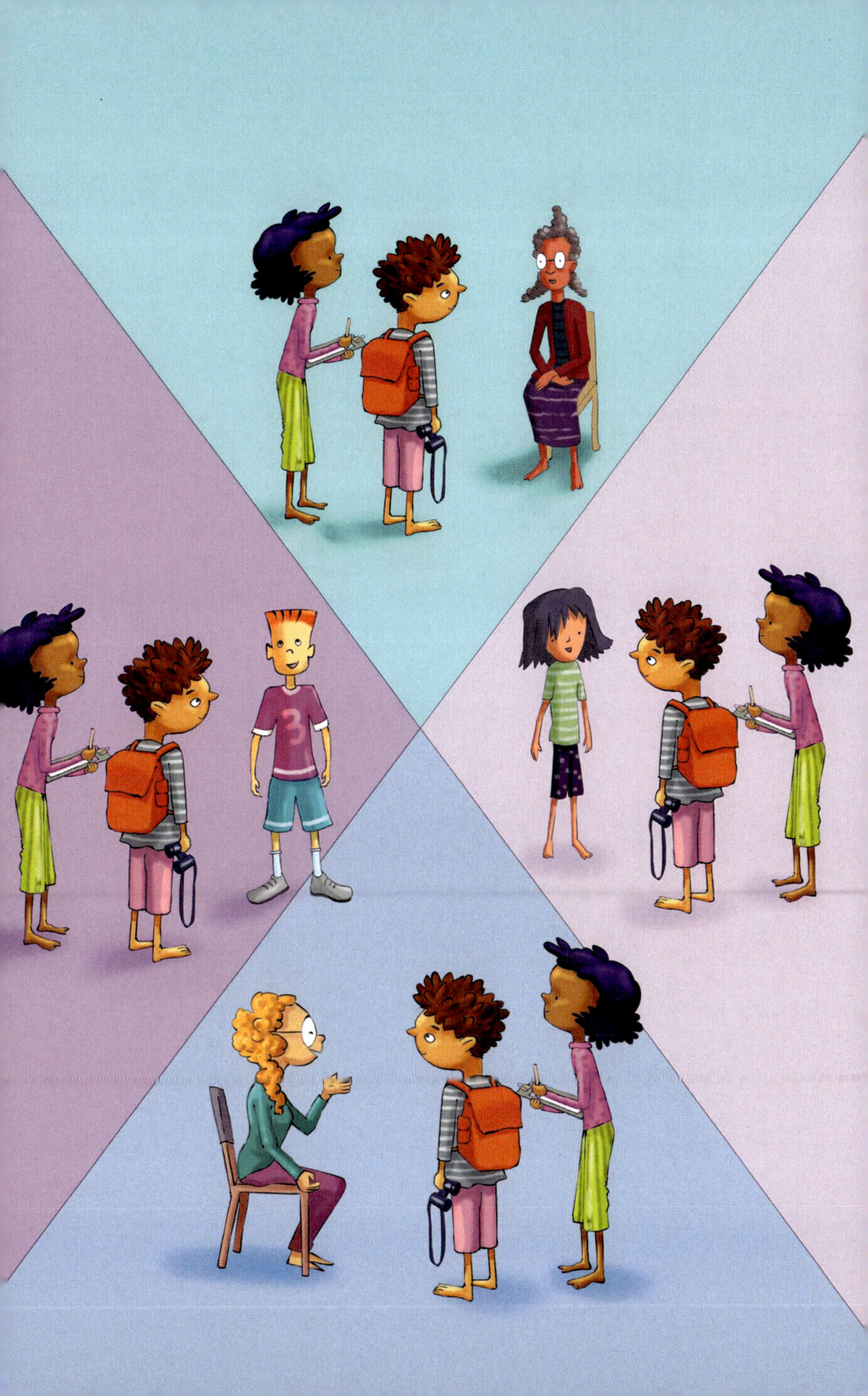

So, first I asked my Gramma.

She said, "It's pretty simple...treat others with care and respect."

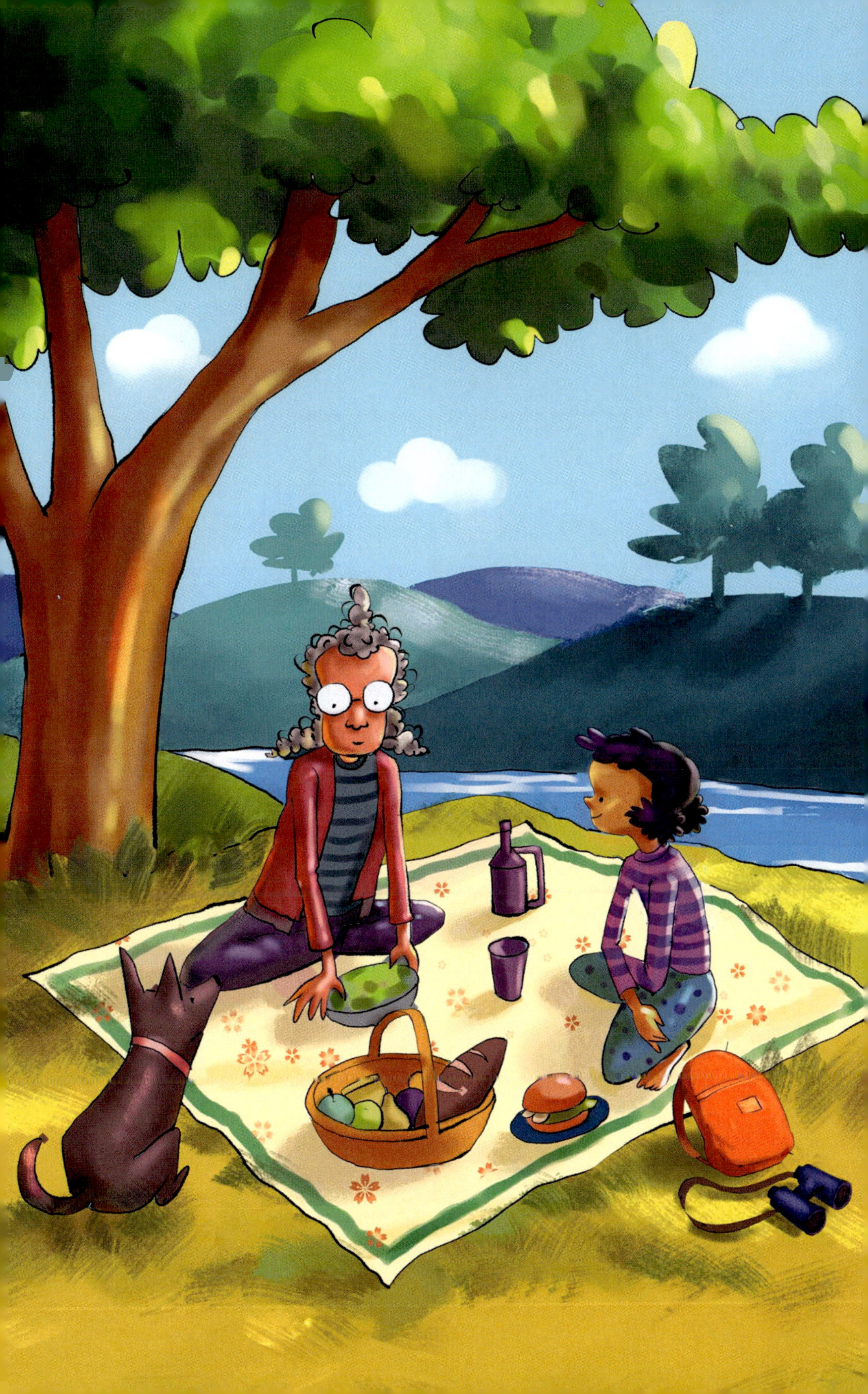

"So...when I give your dog Charlie a lot of love and play with him, that's kidness?", I asked.

Gramma said, "yes, that's a great example, like when you play hide and seek with him!"

Charlie

Then we asked Mom's friend, Mrs. K.

She said, "Kindness means doing things to help another person without expecting anything in return."

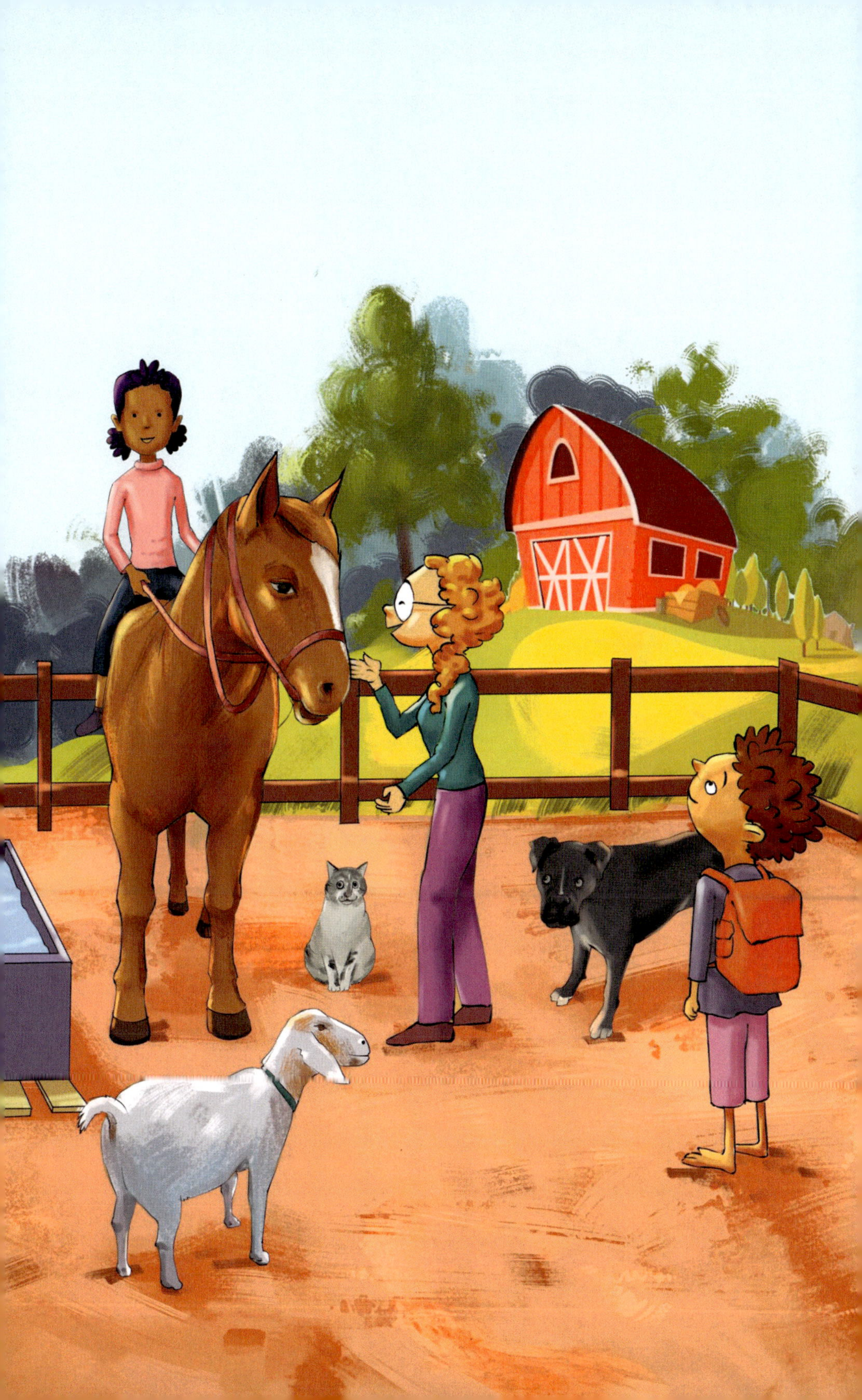

Okay. I get it!

When I help my teacher clean up a mess and don't expect any kind of prize, or anything, then that's kindness.

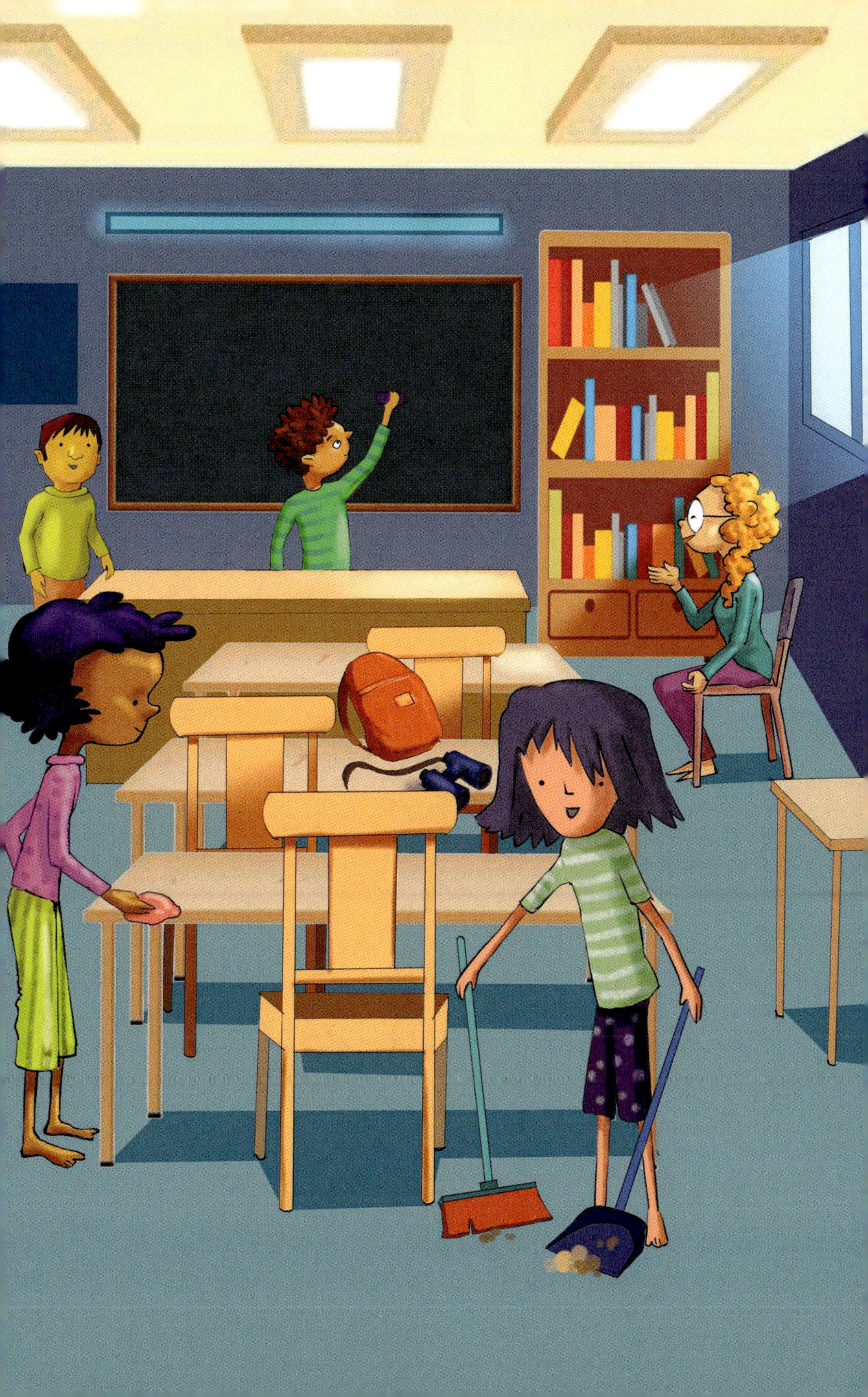

Liam asked his cousin what he thought kindness was.

He said, "Kindness means to be nice and include everyone and to never be mean."

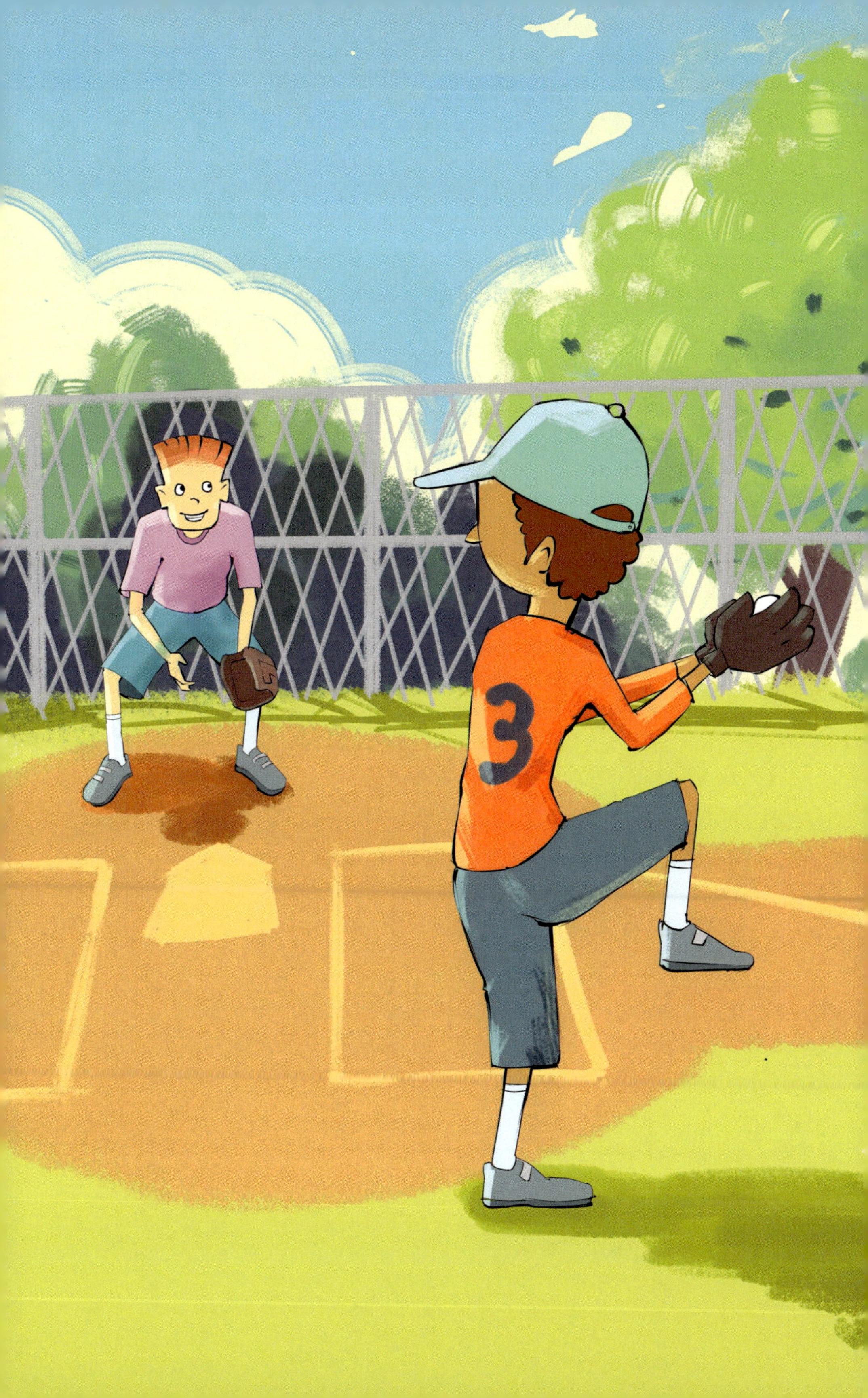

Oh, okay, like the friends I play basketball with? We try to include everyone.

Hmm...I bet there are other kids we can invite to join us. I bet that would make them feel awesome!

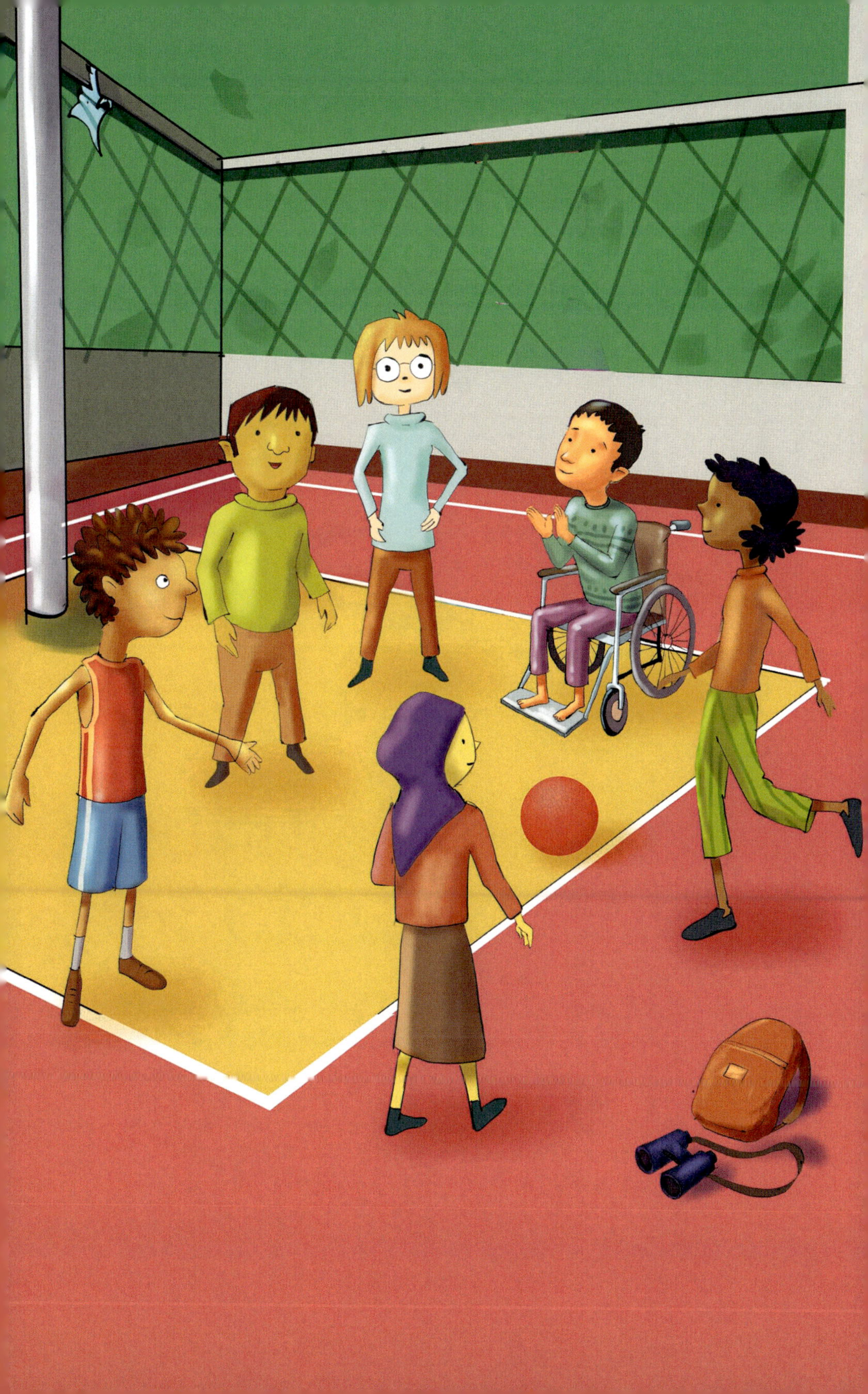

But wait...
Here's one more!
This is from a friend
of ours. We call
her M.K.

She said..."Kindness
means you do the
right thing, even
when nobody is
watching."

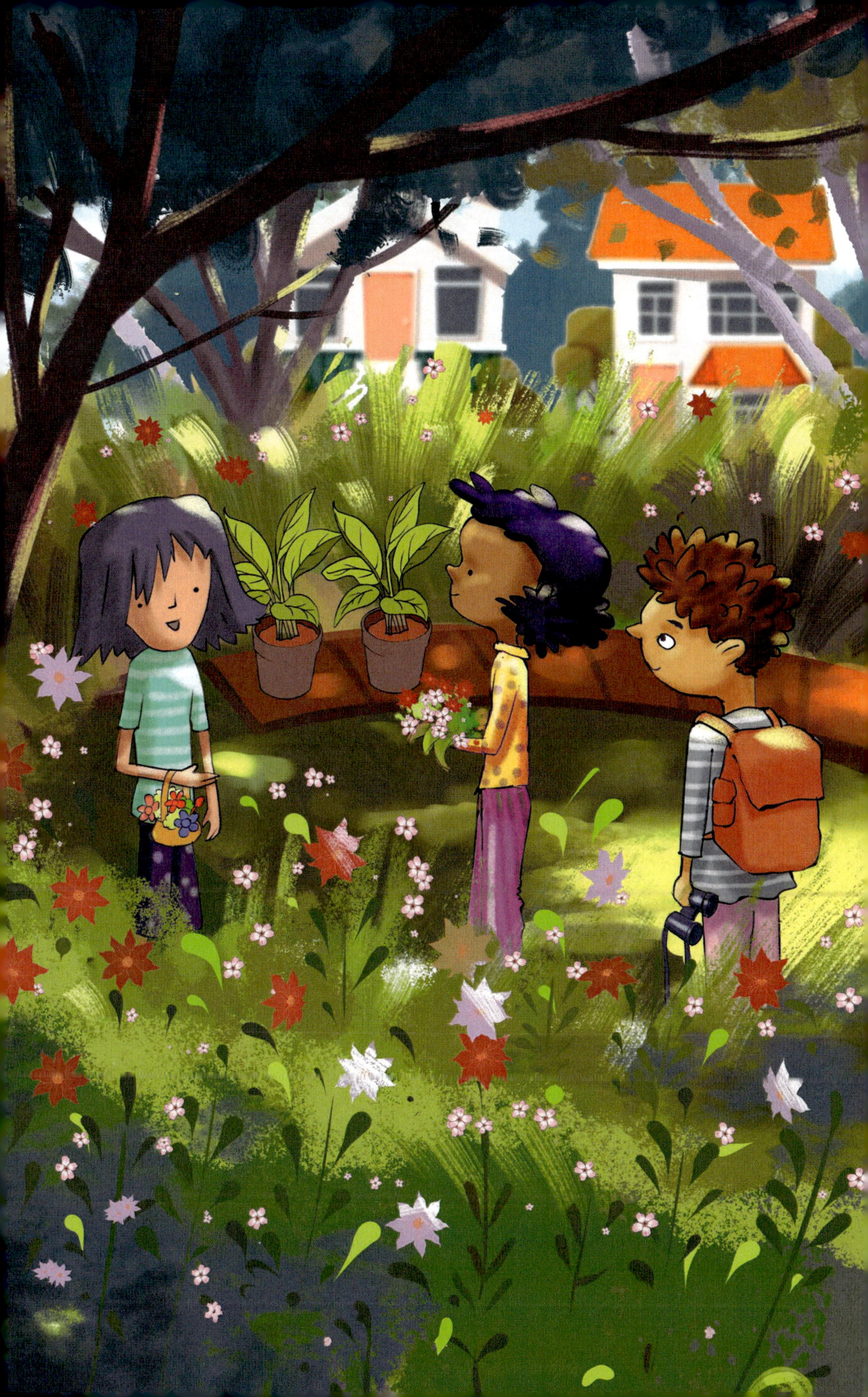

Hey Zuri, remember when we showed kindness by cleaning up the park?
We should do that again. I bet the animals would like that!

Great idea, Liam!

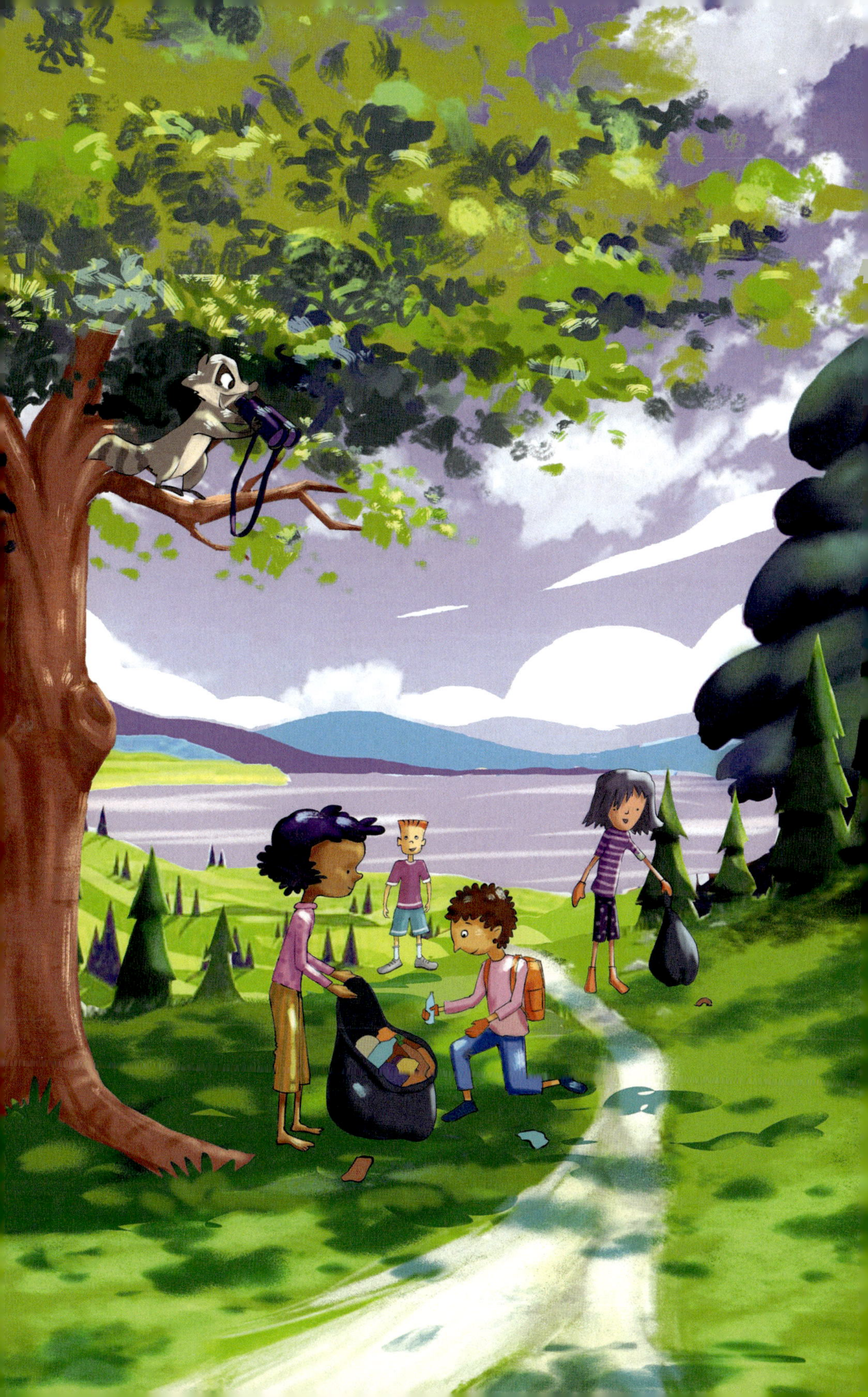

Oh, wow...
I just thought of something else, Zuri.

When we helped that man with his groceries, that was like an act of kindness, and we didn't even realize it!

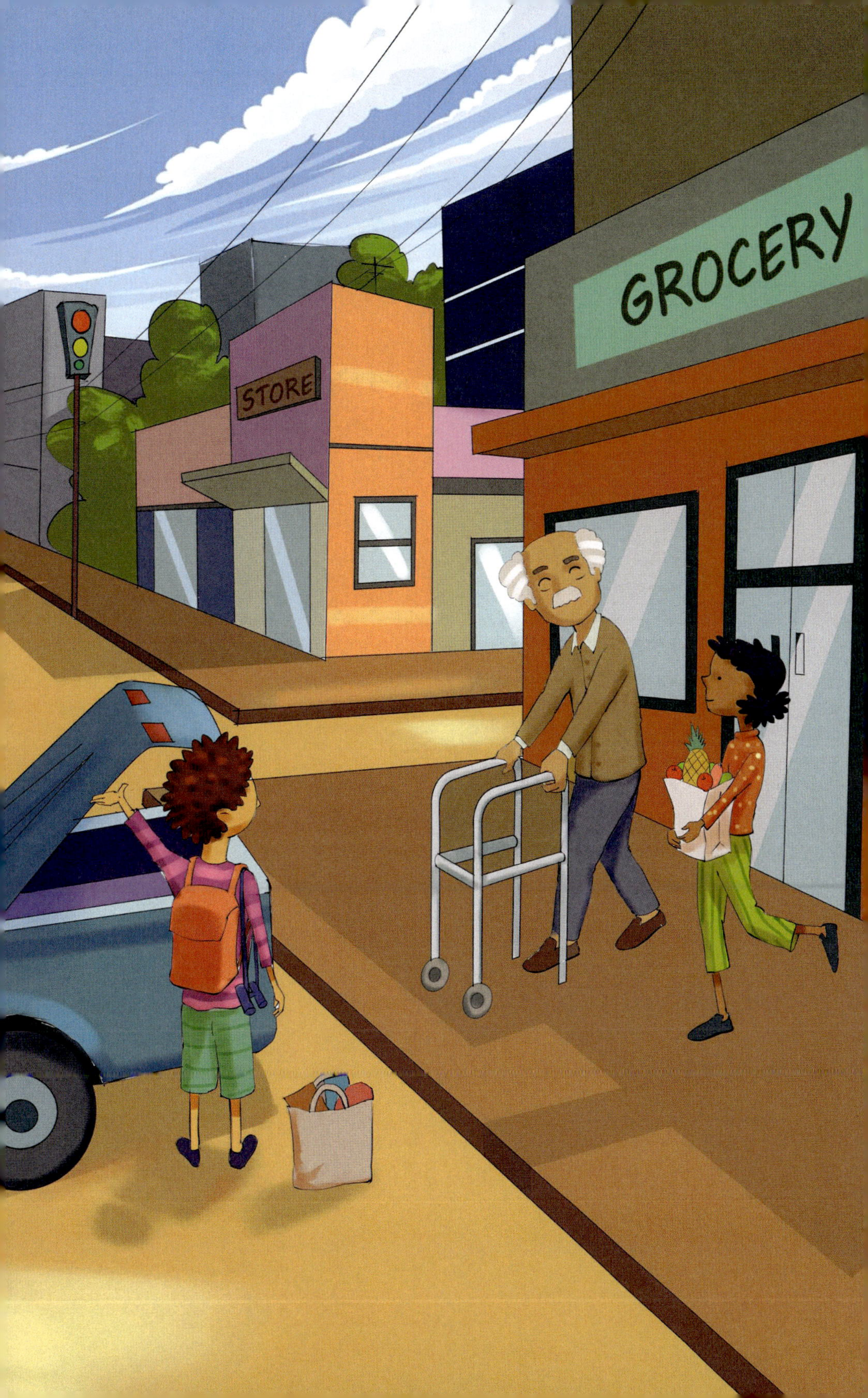
STORE
GROCERY

So...
The information we have gathered shows that being kind means showing care and respect, helping and including others, and doing the right thing, even when no one is watching.

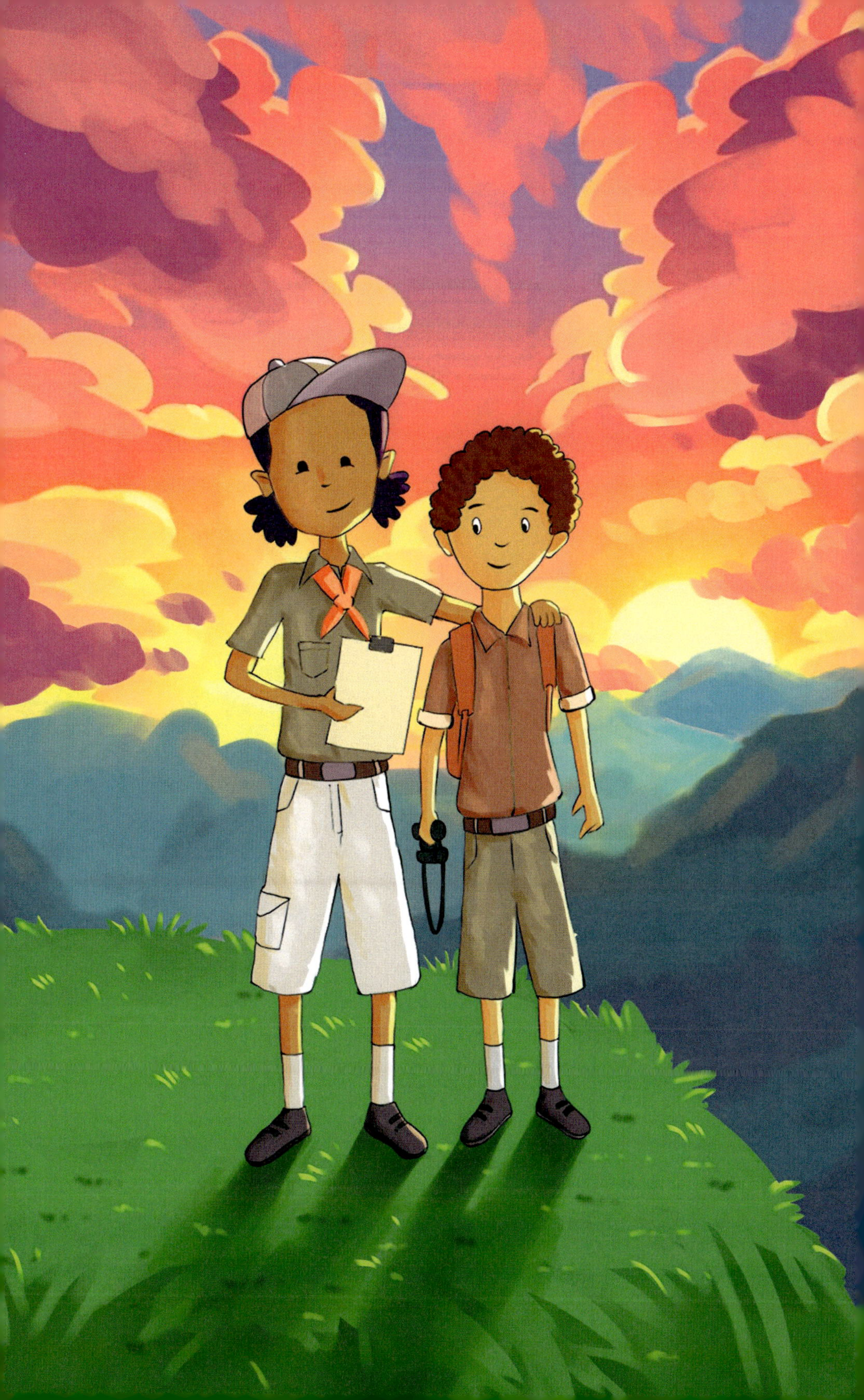

Wow...I never knew how simple kindness could be, Liam.

Our exploring showed us that kindness also makes people happier when they give it and when they receive it! It can possibly change the world!

"Hey"
"Who me"?
"Yeah, I've never seen you before.
"I'm new".
"Oh-my name is Ben. What's yours?
Hi, I'm Joe.
"Let me show you around".

Changing the world...
Let's give it a try.

Do you want
to join us?

When we all work
together, we can
make a
difference!

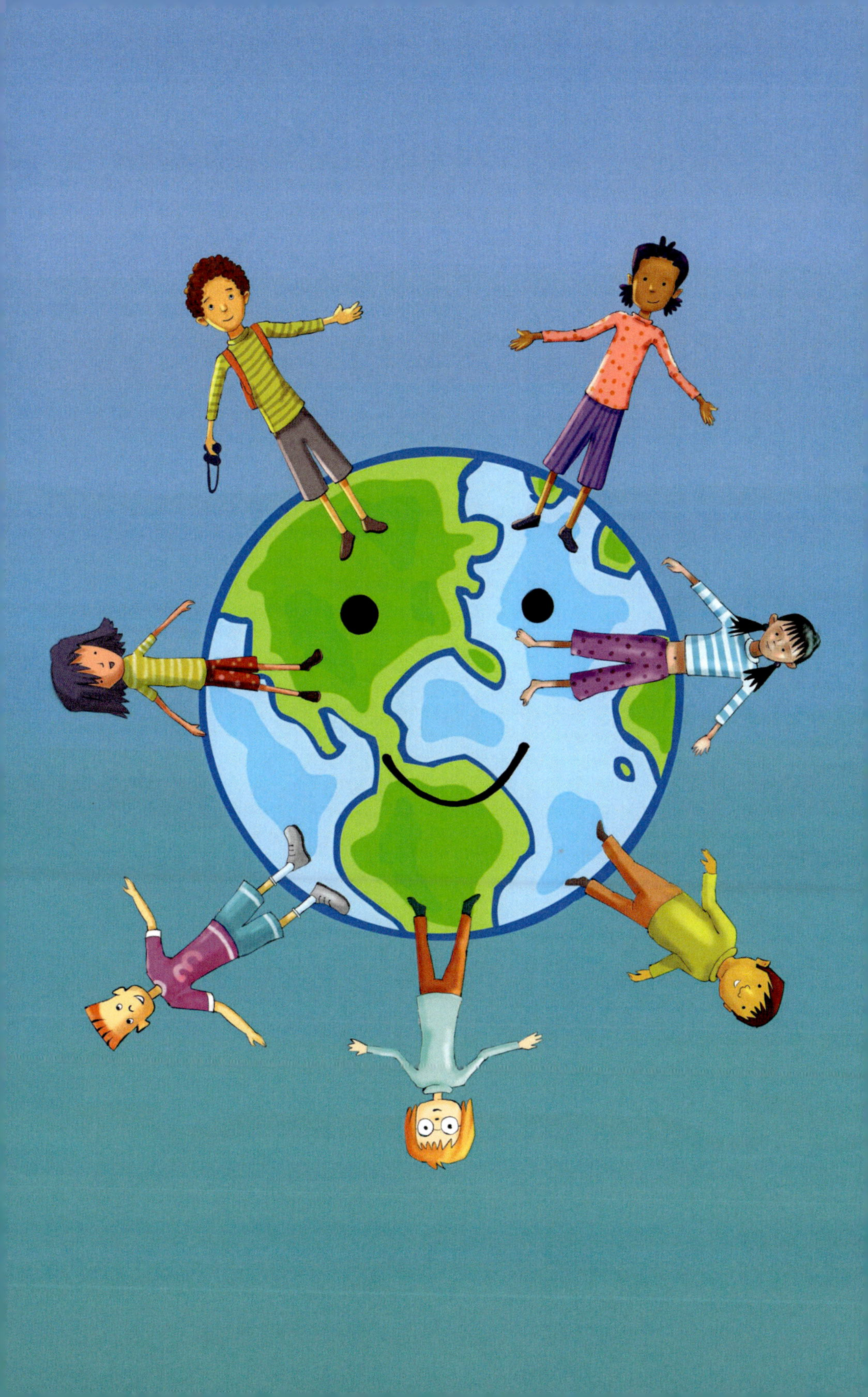

What are some things you can do to spread kindness and change the world in simple ways?

Let's make a list!

kindness list

Hey friends,
did you know that kids just like us are spreading kindness all over the world?

Here are some of their stories.

14 year old Ben cleans up the streets of Malmesbury, Wishire and helps the elderly generation with lawn cutting and technology support.

A student from a school in Texas wanted to make her peers feel good about themselves, so she wrote positive and uplifting notes and stuck them in the bathroom.

Students from the Landlord Elementary Kindness Club visit teachers with their drink cart. It was a big hit and they plan on adding lots of snacks for the teachers to choose from.

Want to read more stories? visit **ripplekindness.org**

Colorado high school senior, Ben, has Down syndrome and is non-verbal. He was nominated for Homecoming King. His classmates, Sarah and Amelia, campaigned for him. When he was crowned as Homecoming King, his classmates chanted, "King Ben!" and cheered him on proudly.

Well, friends, that's it for now!

It was great exploring with you.

We hope you had fun and want to spend time with us again!

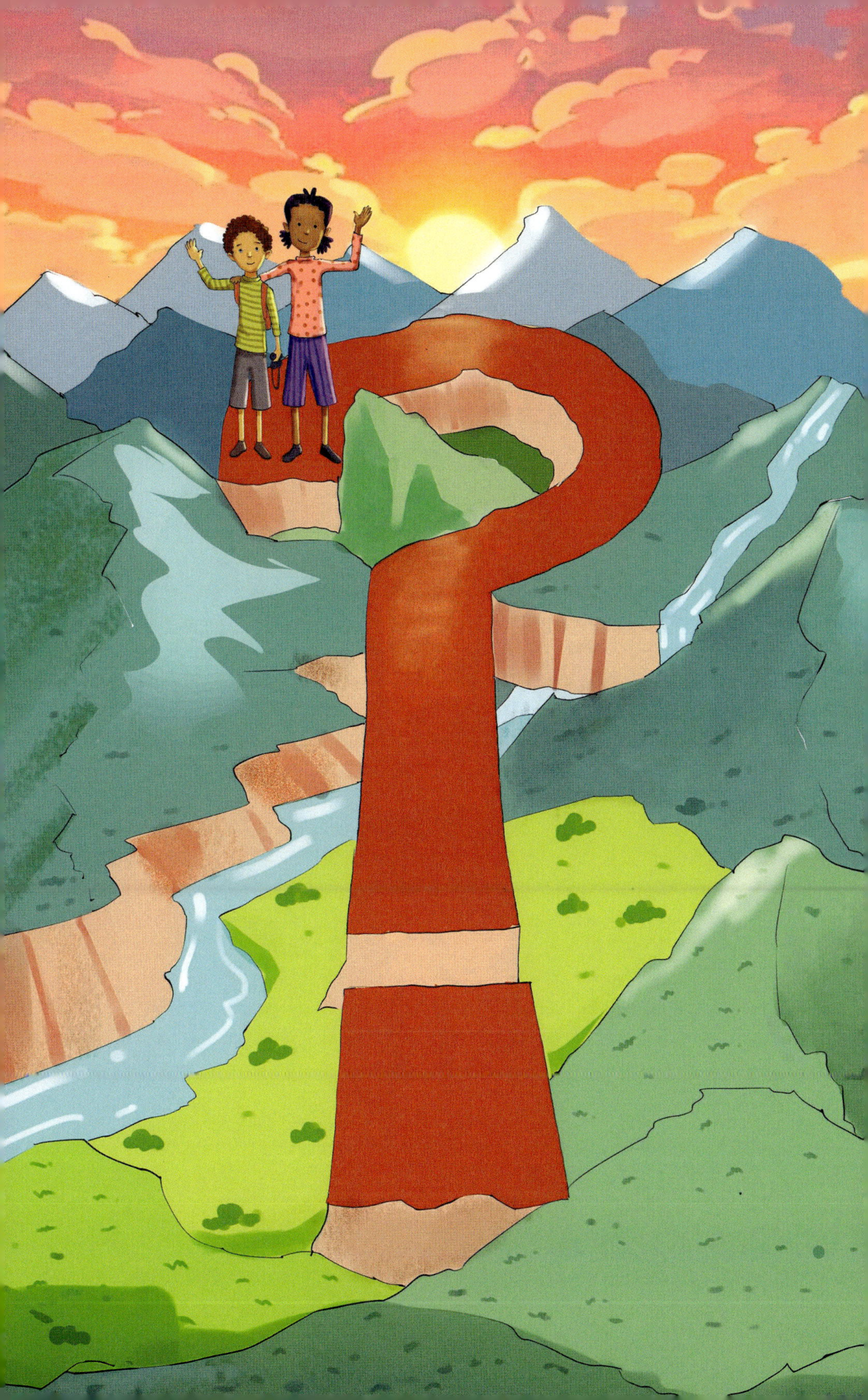

The next time we meet we will be exploring another aspect of kindness... Exploring Differences!

It will be awesome!

Exploration Kindness Series

EXPLORING DIFFERENCES

SUE ALBANESE DAWN KOLTISKA COLEEN THURBER
Illustrated by Partho Roy

Until we meet again, check out the last pages of things you can do right now to show kindness and change the world!

See you soon!

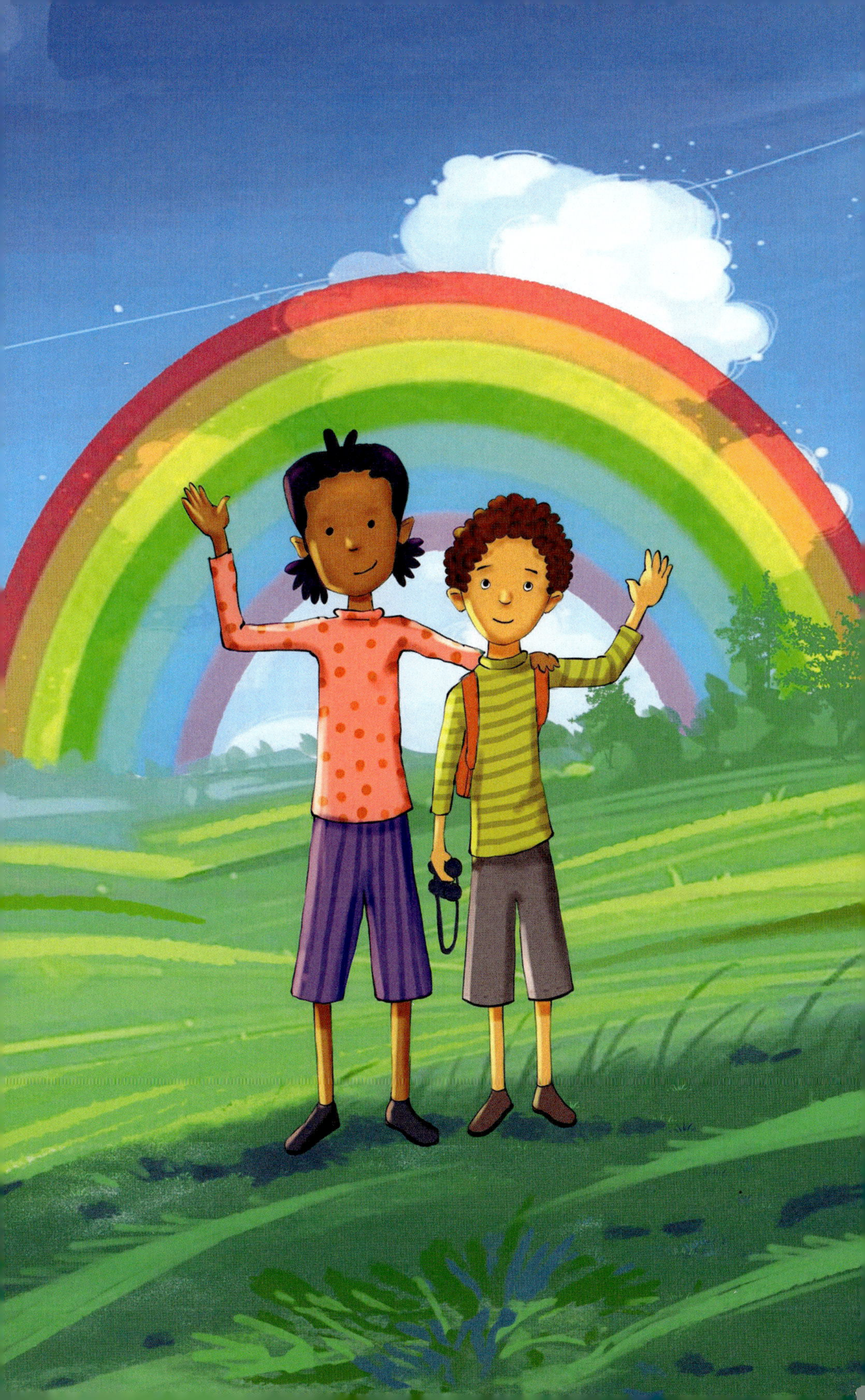

Make a copy of the next page. Add some kind messages to make someone's day. When the time is right, give the gift of a positive message to somebody at your school and watch the kindness spread.

We did a couple for you. Add to them and keep the kindness flowing!

Kindness Notes

Be Happy	Have a great day

Acts of Kindness

1. Let someone have a turn before you.
2. Tell a joke.
3. Check in on an elderly neighbor.
4. Leave happy notes around school or the neighborhood.
5. Make a get well card for someone.
6. Write a poem for a friend.
7. Write a thank you note to the lunch people.
8. Hold the door open for someone.
9. Say hello to everyone you see.
10. Donate a toy to "Toys for Tots".

Acts of Kindness

11. Help make dinner.
12. Leave a letter in a library book.
13. Plant something.
14. Set the table for dinner.
15. Invite somebody to play on the playground.
16. Give compliments to people at school.
17. Teach someone something new.
18. Volunteer to help at school.
19. Help clean the cafeteria.
20. Smile at everyone. It's contagious!

Coming Soon!

The Exploration Kindness Series continues!

Keep an eye out for more adventures in learning as Zuri and Liam explore powerful topics, such as Differences, Words, Disabilities… and more.

Exploration **Kindness**

Follow us:

Facebook:
https://www.facebook.com/explorationkindness/

Instagram:
@exploration_kindness

About the Authors

Sue Albanese, PhD is a retired Air Force veteran who served our great country for 28 years. As a registered behavioral therapist, Sue spent many years as a para educator in various elementary schools working with children with moderate to severe needs. Sue has a doctorate degree in Psychology, and is the primary caregiver to both her senior mom and special needs son. Born in Illinois, Sue moved to Colorado in 1982. Sue is a proud mother of two adult children, Maggie and Ben, and the honored Aunt of Becky and Melissa. Sue's passion lies in helping others and considers herself an eternal optimist - believing in the possibility of a kinder world. Sue was inspired to write this book because of her great nieces and nephew, Brady, Riley, and Jaxon. Her hope is that they, as well as all children, will learn to be the best version of themselves and spread kindness daily.

Dawn Koltiska is a licensed clinical school social worker in Aurora, Colorado. For 25 years she has been a respected and integral part of the mental health team in the Cherry Creek School District. Born and raised in Wyoming, Dawn has spent most of her adult life in Colorado. She is the proud mother of three awesome children and one wonderful granddaughter, and has many fur babies that inhabit her homestead in Franktown, Colorado. Dawn considers herself an advocate for social change and justice and has worked tirelessly to make the world a better place for all children. She is thrilled to co-write this set of chidren's books.

Coleen Thurber is proud to be a retired elementary school teacher of 30 years. She has dedicated an entire career to teaching children the power of kindness and coaching her students to be the best humans they can be! Through the creation of her own character education program, she has inspired thousands of her students to live a life of great character. Coleen is also incredibly honored to wear the title of "Mom" to her awesome 9- and 12-year-old boys who completely rock her world. Although born and raised in Massachusetts, Coleen has called Colorado home for the past 25 years. She shares her life adventure with her wonderful husband, her two amazings sons, and the world's cutest labradoodle. Whether in school, at home, or in the neighborhood, Coleen consideres herself a champion for kids of all ages. The Exploration Kindness Series has been such a beautiful collaboration amongst friends and an opportunity to emplower kids to be their greatest self.

Made in the USA
Middletown, DE
14 December 2024